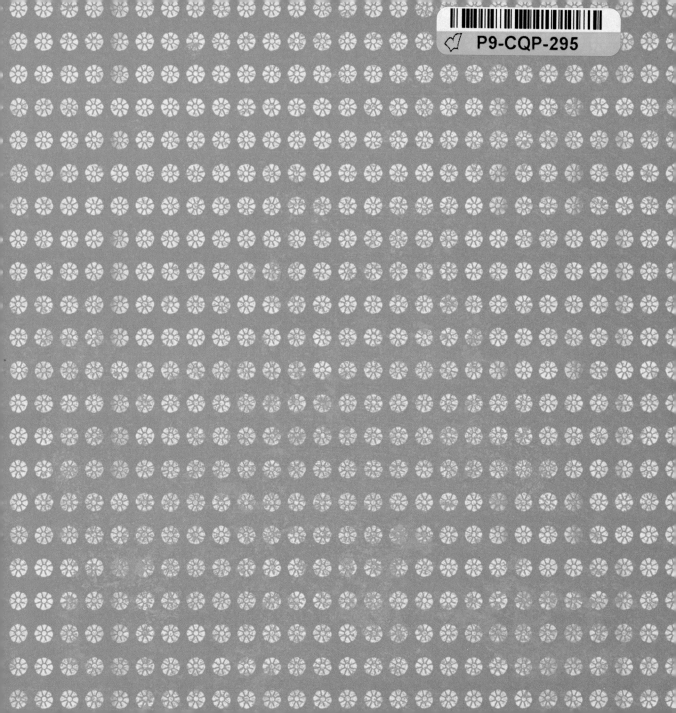

Let's Work!

Mexican Folk Art Trabajos in English and Spanish

Cynthia Weill and Bryant Boucher
Palm Weavings from Puebla by
Master Artisans of Chigmecatitlán

Let's work! What do you want to be?
¡Vamos a trabajar! ¿Qué quieres ser?

You can be a painter,
Puedes ser pintor o pintora,

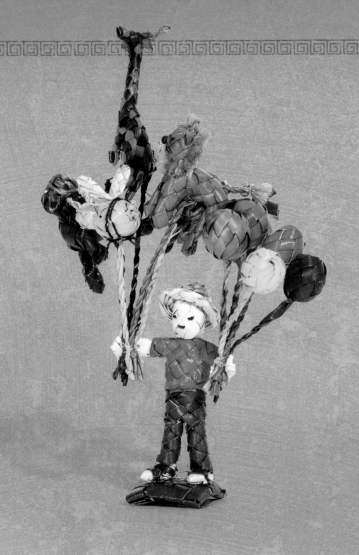

a balloon seller,
vendedor o vendedora de globos,

a cowboy or a cowgirl,
vaquero o vaquera,

or an equestrian.
o jinete.

You can be a clown,
Puedes ser payasa o payaso,

a dancer,
bailarina o bailarín,

a gardener,
jardinero o jardinera,

or a hair dresser.
o peluquera o peluquero.

You can be a nurse,
Puedes ser enfermera o enfermero,

a doctor,
doctora o doctor,

a chef,
chef,

or a waitress or a waiter.
o mesera o mesero.

You can be a bike racer,

Puedes ser ciclista,

a boxer,
boxeadora o boxeador,

a carpenter,
carpintera o carpintero,

or an electrician.

o electricista.

You can be a teacher,
Puedes ser maestra o maestro,

a librarian,
bibliotecaria o bibliotecario,

a photographer,
fotógrafo o fotógrafa,

or a musician.
o música o músico.

You can be a soccer player,
Puedes ser futbolista,

a jockey,
jockey,

a fisherman or fisherwoman,
pescador o pescadora,

or work with computers.
o trabajar con computadoras.

You can be a taxi driver,
Puedes ser taxista,

put out fires,
apagar fuegos,

play baseball,

jugar al béisbol,

or be another type of athlete.
o ser otro tipo de deportista.

You can be so many things.
Puedes ser tantas cosas.

What work will you choose?
¿Cuál trabajo piensas elegir?

The miniature palm weavings in *Let's Work!* were made by master artisans in the village of Chigmecatitlán in the Mixteca region of the Mexican state of Puebla. Most pieces are slightly larger than a coin. It takes tremendous skill and patience to weave each one. The artisans of this region have been making this craft since before the arrival of the Spanish in the early 16th century.

The Artisans / los artesanos

Mauro Ríos Payán, María Verónica Peralta Ordóñez, Judith Beltrán Campos, Silvia Gallardo Osorio, Zahira Guadalupe Palacios Gallardo, Basilia Micaela Sánchez Pineda, Flavio Gallardo Osorio, Rosario Peralta Ordóñez, Macedonia Campos Ramiro, Jesús Ángel Gallardo Sánchez, Saúl Naín Peralta Ordóñez. (Not shown: Laura Gallardo Osorio)

Dedication

To Victoria Weill and Bruce Boucher, ¡los queremos mucho!

Very Special Thanks to

Flavio Gallardo Osorio, master artisan of Chigmecatitlán, Puebla, who helped make this book a reality.

Thanks to

Anne Mayagoitia, Ruth Meyers, Jorge Herrera Olvera, Ruth Borgman, Nancy Mygatt, Catherine Boucher, The Bank Street Writers Lab, Museo Estatal de Artes Populares de Oaxaca, Carlomagno Pedro Martínez, Fernando Pedro Fabián, Casa Panchita, Bryant Boucher, Myriam Chapman, The Field Museum of Chicago, Alexander Boucher, Melissa Boucher, Nicholas Boucher

Cover and Book Design by Sergio A. Gómez

Identifiers: LCCN 2018964193| ISBN 978-1-947627-15-4 (hardback)
LC record available at http://lccn.loc.gov/2018964193